The Malhata Fortress on the Roman-Judaean Negev Frontier: Associated with a Roman Road, the Frankincense Trail, and a Princely Fugitive

Echoes of Ancient Rome: Politics, Medicine, and War

Elizabeth Legge

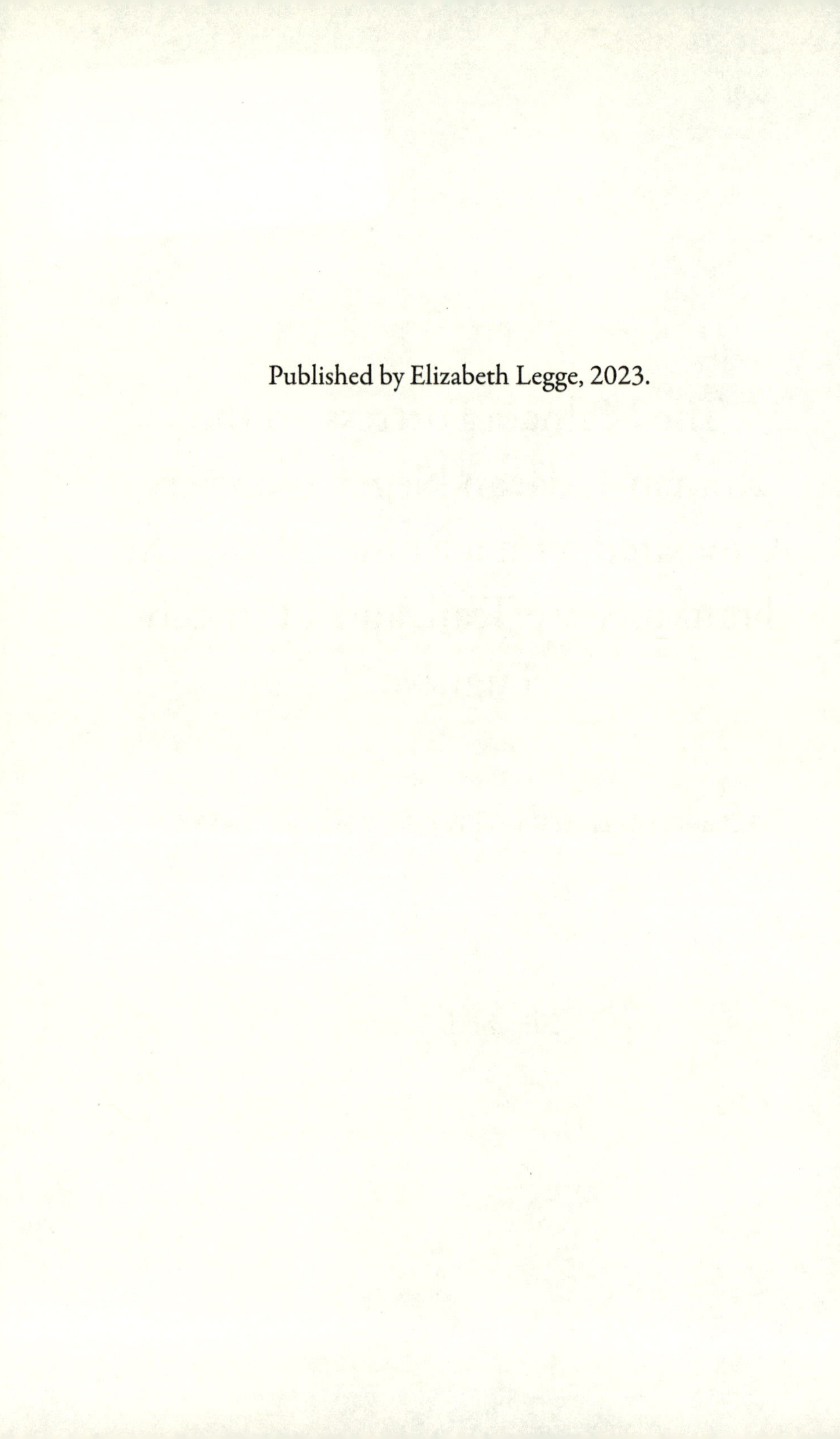

Published by Elizabeth Legge, 2023.

THE MALHATA FORTRESS ON THE ROMAN-JUDAEAN NEGEV FRONTIER: ASSOCIATED WITH A ROMAN ROAD, THE FRANKINCENSE TRAIL, AND A PRINCELY FUGITIVE

First edition. December 2, 2023.

ISBN: 979-8230071846

Written by Elizabeth Legge.

Also by Elizabeth Legge

Echoes of Ancient Rome: Politics, Medicine, and War
Woman Physicians in Ancient Rome
The Structure and Phases of the Castra Praetoria in Rome
Roman Military Medicine from an Archaeological and Historical
Perspective
Gaius Caligula's Reign, Personality and Friendship with M. Julius
Agrippa I
The Malhata Fortress on the Roman-Judaean Negev Frontier:
Associated with a Roman Road, the Frankincense Trail, and a Princely
Fugitive
Agrippa I: A Comprehensive Archaeological Study of the Last King of
Roman Judaea and a True Crime Inquiry

Roman Provincial Shadows: Agrippa I, Intrigue, and Power
Herodian Agrippa I Archaeology: Introduction
Historical Background for Herodian Agrippa I
Fugitive Prince: The Negev Hideout of Agrippa I at Malhata
Examples for Comparison from Herod I's Archaeological Record
Agrippa I: An Archaeological Biography of the Last King of Roman
Judaea
Agrippa I's Last Days

Herodian Agrippa I Archaeology: Discussion, Conclusion and Reference List

Table of Contents

My heartfelt thanks to my mother, whose immense knowledge of ancient history and archaeology, along with her introducing me since early childhood to the world of international adventure travel, has shaped my passions profoundly. Her unwavering support has been instrumental in my research on this all-encompassing subject. And to my best friend, Patricia McBride, whose steadfast companionship and encouragement have been invaluable throughout my journey—I am profoundly grateful.

Many thanks as well to Dr. Anthony Barrett, renowned Roman historian and former professor of mine at the University of British Columbia, who peer-reviewed this work and recommended it for publication at *Roman Roads Itinera* journal, and to *Roman Roads Itinera* for publishing it first.

"Fortune sides with him who dares." – Virgil, *Aeneid*

"...he retired to a certain tower, at Malatha..." – Josephus, *Antiquities* 18.6.147

The Malhata Fortress on the Roman-Judaean Negev Frontier: Associated with a Roman Road, the Frankincense Trail, and a Princely Fugitive

by Elizabeth Legge

Abstract

MALHATA IS ONE OF A group of fortresses on the Roman-Judaean frontier with Nabataea (roughly equivalent to modern Jordan). This fortress, located on a tel in the southern portion of the group, is associated with the remains of a Roman road and occupied a strategically central position on an important crossroads between southern Roman Palestine and central Judaea, and between the Dead and Mediterranean seas. It was also on the Roman sector of the Frankincense Trail caravan trade route with the Arabian Peninsula. As well, it is believed to have been 'Malatha', mentioned by the Roman- Jewish historian Josephus as the location where the fugitive Herodian prince, Agrippa I, hid when forced to flee his privileged life in Rome among the Julio-Claudians. An archaeological excavation report and GIS spatial analysis of Malhata reveal information on the fortress' purpose, and support its being the location where Agrippa hid.

Previously published in *Itinera*, Vol. 3, 2023

Introduction

Marcus Julius Agrippa I, the grandson of Herod the Great, was an adventurous and colourful character skilled at intrigue and mentioned in both the *Book of Acts* and by

the historian, Flavius Josephus. He grew up in Rome with the children of the Julio-Claudians and close friends with Caesar Tiberius' son and heir apparent, Drusus, and his career then was very promising. However, shortly after Drusus' sudden death at the hands – it was later discovered – of the praetorian prefect, Lucius Aelius Sejanus, he fled Rome and hid in a tower at Malatha. How does this historical action thriller and crime mystery connect with a Judaean Roman road?

Figure 1, for clarity, is a map of Roman-Herodian Judaea as it was during the first half of the first century AD before the reign of Agrippa I but during the period of his stay at Malatha and in the Galilee as mentioned in this article. The Negev, the location of *Malhata* fortress and the fortress group referred to in this article, roughly comprises Roman *Idumaea*, the Herodian

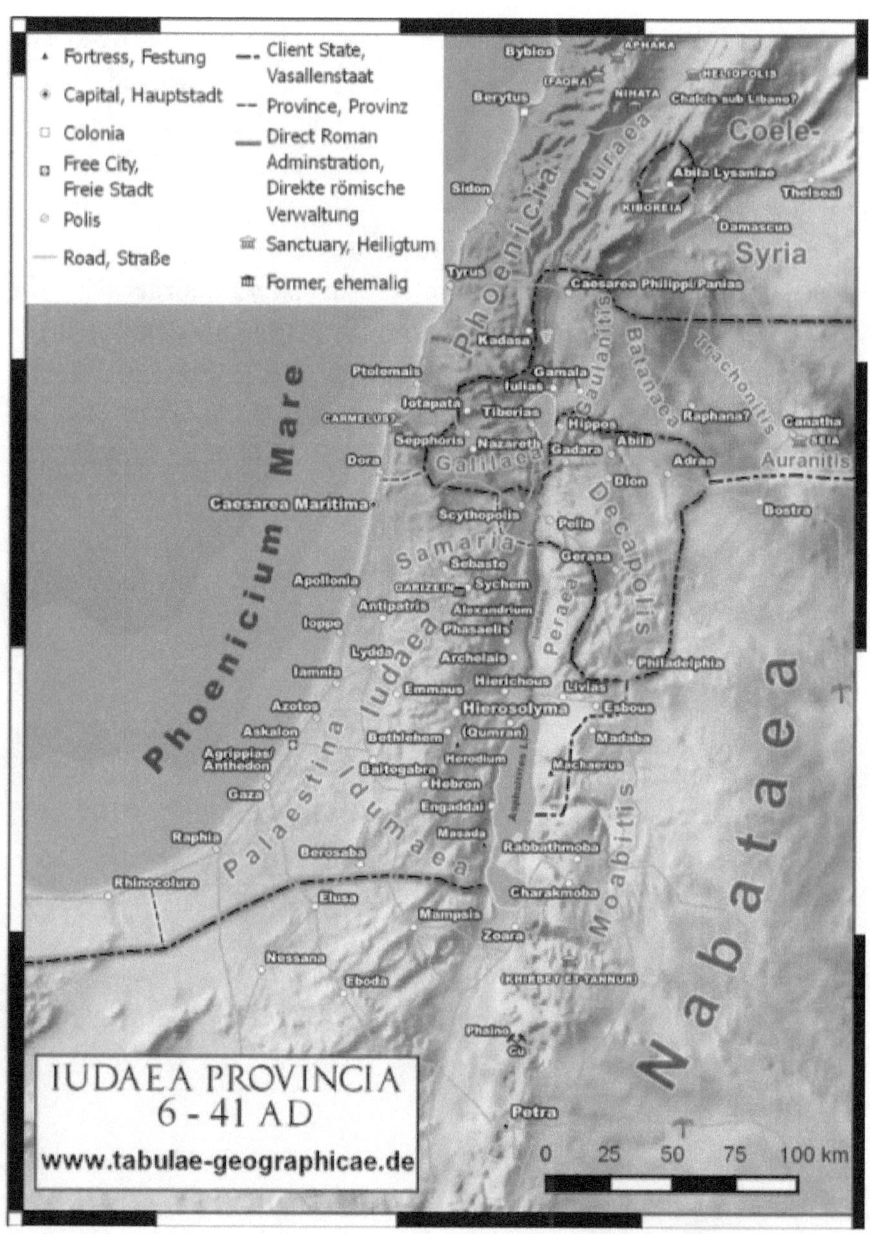

Figure 1. Map of Herodian Judaea and the Decapolis (Ditter, M. The First Province of Judea, n.d., n.p.; courtesy of *Tabulae Geographicae*, n.d. n.p.)

FAMILY'S ANCESTRAL home. This area is west of the Dead Sea, and *Malhata* is near Hebron. *Tiberias*, where Agrippa later worked for and acquired intelligence on his uncle, the tetrarch Antipas, is Antipas' city in the province of Galilee, north of *Idumaea*, *Judaea* and *Samaria*, and just west of the Sea of Galilee.

Archaeologically, a group of Roman fortresses used for policing and later as a *limes* have been found on Roman *Judaea*'s border with the wealthy Arabian kingdom of *Nabataea*, which roughly comprised the area now known as Jordan. Figure 2 displays the area in which *Malhata* and the surrounding group of Negev fortresses referred to here are located. The location of the actual fortress group is bounded by the red box. Some of these fortresses, positioned in the southern portion in the Judaean Negev,

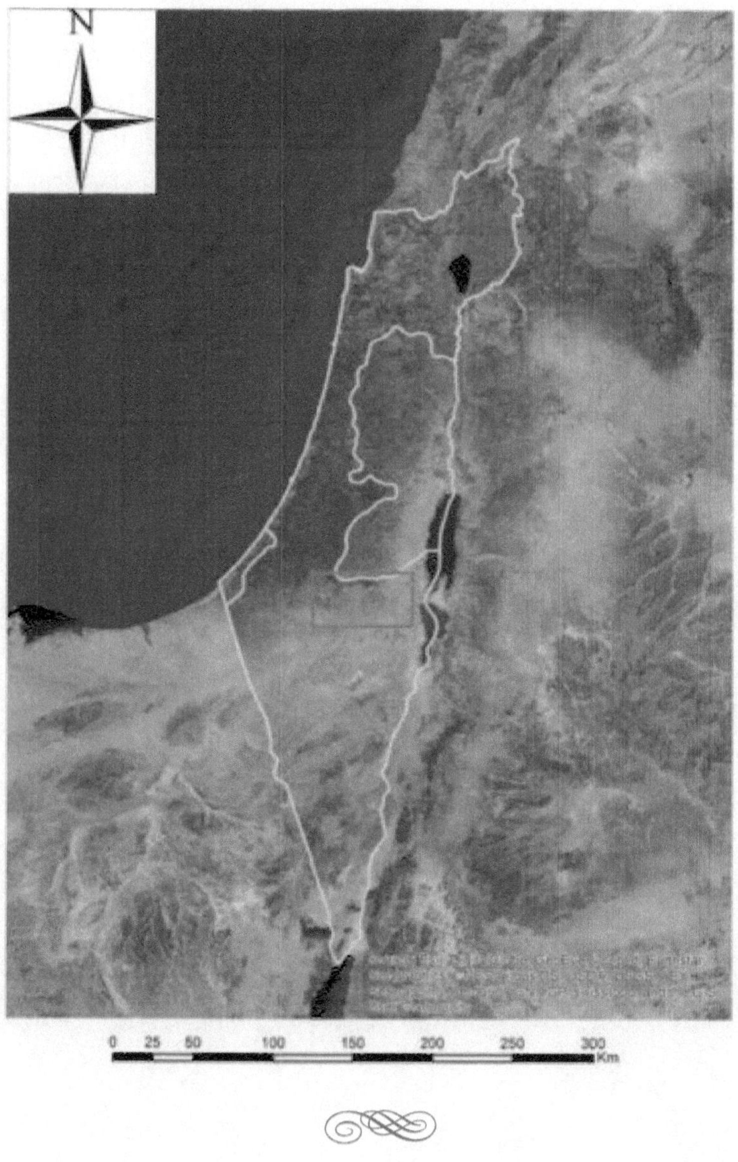

Figure 2. Map of area of Negev's Roman fortresses in Judaea (Pazout, A., 2018, 174, Fig. 1; courtesy of the author)

SEEM TO HAVE GUARDED the Roman Empire's sector of the Frankincense Trail, and these include the Fortress of *Malhata*. The remains of a Roman road were found near this fortress. This stronghold is particularly interesting for a couple of reasons. First of all, it is believed to have been Josephus' *Malatha* tower where Agrippa fled. Secondly, this strategically connected defensive structure, located at an important crossroads in Roman Palestine, may have guarded a caravanserai. I shall be discussing how this tower relates to Josephus' action story regarding Agrippa, some historical possibilities for why the Roman-Judaean prince was really hiding there, how the archaeological remains and their dating suggest that this was Josephus' *Malatha* tower, information on the Roman road and important crossroads associated with this fortress, and some interesting features of the fortress itself including its importance in the Negev frontier fortress group. Its archaeological remains will be discussed as they substantiate the historical material.

Agrippa I's Early Days: The Historical Background and a Roman Murder Mystery

Let us begin with the early first century AD historical background. M. Julius Agrippa had an Imperial education, and as the grandson of Herod I and his Hasmonean/Maccabean Jewish queen, Mariamne, and the good friend of Drusus, was an excellent candidate for a highly successful political career (Josephus. *Antiquities*, 18.143-6). Although the Herods were apparently good friends as well as clients of the Julio-Claudians, Agrippa I seems to have been even closer to the Julio-Claudians than the other Herods were and more than a mere client king in terms of his privilege and closeness to those who were to become the next emperors of Rome (Josephus, 18.143-6, 224-37, 289-97, 19.236-44, etc.; Curran 2014, 505- 6). Later events show that he was very knowledgeable about Roman political intricacies and the operation of the Empire's government (Josephus, 18.224-37, 289-97, 19.236-244, etc.; Kropp 2013, 379-80), and that he afterwards achieved an extremely influential position with the emperor Gaius 'Caligula', who gave him the first portion of his Judaean kingdom (Josephus, 18.224-237, 245-56, 289-304, etc.; Cassius Dio, lix, 24). He also played a significant role in Claudius' subsequent achievement of the Principate (Josephus, 19.236-44; Kropp 2013, 378). However, at this earlier stage, he suddenly faced a crisis: Drusus died very suddenly in AD 23, and eight years later, in AD 31, Antonia Minor informed the emperor Tiberius that his next-in-command, his trusted praetorian prefect and friend, Sejanus, had been involved in conspiracy against him (Josephus, 18.181-2), and it was afterwards revealed that Sejanus had murdered Tiberius' heir, Drusus (Cassius Dio, lviii.11). It would not be unreasonable to suggest that Antonia's warning to Tiberius might also have revealed Sejanus' involvement in the assassination (Kokkinos 1998, 275). Why did it take so long for this information on Drusus' murder to surface? First, I shall examine the events which immediately followed the assassination.

Figure 3 allows the reader to better visualise Agrippa, on which this article focuses. This modern sculpture, found in the Israel Museum in Jerusalem, reconstructs his appearance from his clearest coin, minted when he achieved his kingdom, and demonstrates his Romanised appearance and apparent identification. Note that he wears a diadem, signifying his kingship status.

FIGURE 3. SCULPTURE reconstruction of the head of Agrippa I, modelled after his best- preserved coin, demonstrating his presentation as Roman or classical. (Courtesy of the Israel Museum, Jerusalem, Israel)

Upon the death of Augustus' designated heir, Germanicus, Tiberius began to clearly mark out Drusus, rather than Germanicus' sons, as his heir. This was made apparent when Drusus first shared the consulship with his father in AD 21 and was then granted tribunician status in AD 22 (Shaw 1990, p. ii; Tacitus. *Annals*, III). It was shortly after this, in AD 23, that Drusus unexpectedly died. With this occurrence, Agrippa suddenly lost both his male patron (Drusus) and all prospects for his career. Despite his spending much of his limited inheritance on gifts to Imperial freedmen to negotiate for his career and attempt to arrange meetings with Tiberius, he was barred from the emperor's presence on the official pretext that Tiberius was mourning his son and did not wish to be painfully reminded of him by meeting his friends (Josephus, 18.143-50). Now, Antonia Minor was Agrippa's only patron, and he lacked employment. Agrippa had also, according to the official story, spent the last of his inheritance on fruitless attempts at networking and was being pursued by various creditors (Josephus, 18.143- 50). He therefore had no choice but to flee to *Judaea*, which he had probably not seen since he was around five years of age, and hide at or near the remote *Malatha* desert fortress in *Idumaea* (the Negev). The Herods being an Idumaean family, he may have had an obscure family property near *Malatha*. Applebaum (1967, qtd. in Tal 2015b, 18; Pazout 2015, 50) suggests the 'tower' Josephus speaks of was an agricultural tower or fortified estate house which may have belonged to an old Idumaean family property. Similar such properties have been identified in outlying parts of Roman Palestine (Tal 2015b, 18; Pazout 2015, 50). Agrippa's flight took place, it is believed, in the late AD 20s, at the time of Sejanus' rise to power.

Agrippa in Judaea and Syria

Agrippa remained in Judaea and Syria until the early AD 30s. In *Malatha*, as one who identified as Roman, he became so depressed and perhaps also shamed from his turn of fortune, he contemplated suicide (but was saved from carrying this out by his caring wife, Cypros). After a little while, however, in the early 30s AD (Schwartz 1990, 46-47; Kokkinos 1998, 273), he found employment with his uncle, Antipas the tetrarch of Galilee (Josephus, 18.147). He used the opportunity to spy on his ambitious uncle and gather useful intelligence on the man's questionable dealings with Parthia (Roman era Persia). This power was the arch-enemy of Rome; therefore, one of the Herods' main purposes as a Roman ruling family in *Judaea* was to be a protective Roman political presence in the Parthian buffer zone. Antipas had also amassed an enormous secret arsenal. He then fled to his friend, Flaccus', protection in Syria and, when that was no longer offered, hurried by rented boat – narrowly evading arrest – to Antonia's agent in Alexandria, Egypt and then back to Italy. He was immediately welcomed – rather than shunned as before – by Tiberius on Capri and, with Antonia's help, found employment with him (Josephus, 18.147-60). Following Tiberius' death, he became one of Caligula's right-hand men and used the intelligence gathered on Antipas to achieve that tetrarch's exile and the second part of his kingdom (Josephus, 18.245-56; Legge 2021).

Agrippa and Intrigue

The position that the tetrarch of Galilee, Antipas, had given Agrippa was that of *agoronomos* (Roman *aedile*) or overseer of the marketplace in Antipas' city of *Tiberias* (Josephus, 18.147- 50; Meyers & Mark 2012, 124). A lead weight found at Tiberias is engraved as belonging to an *agoronomos* named Gaius Julius who held this position in AD 30/31 during the thirty-fourth year of the reign of Antipas (Stein 1992, 144-45).

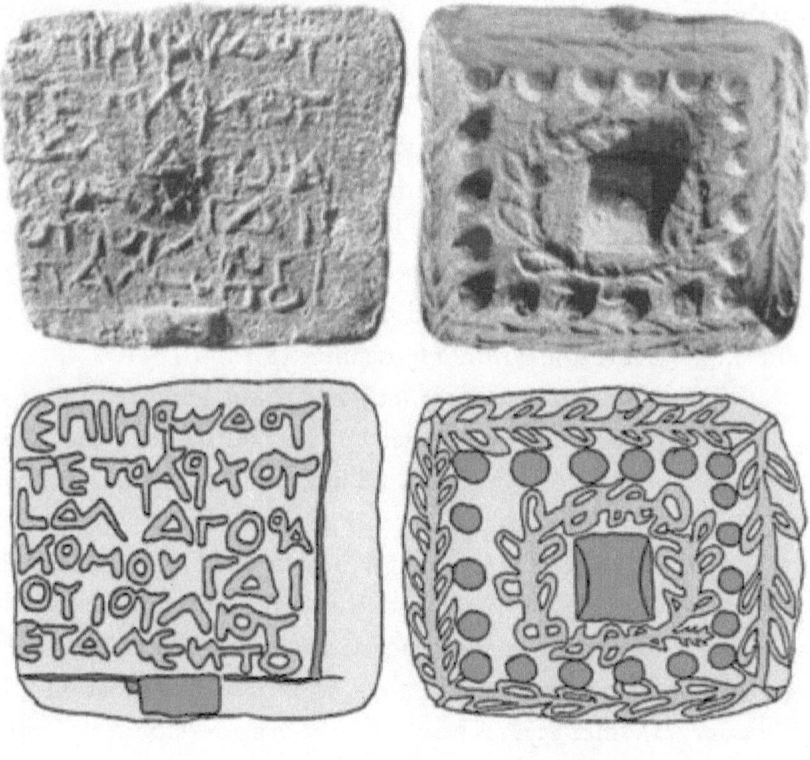

Figure 4. Weight found at Tiberias inscribed with the name of the *agoronomos*, Gaius Julius, and dated to AD 30/31 (Kogon, A. & Fontanille, J.-P., 2018, n.p. Fig. 7.1); courtesy of the authors

THIS WAS UNLIKELY TO have been Agrippa: it is nearly certain that his *praenomen* (Roman first name) was Marcus, since he had been named for the statesman, Marcus Vipsanius Agrippa, Augustus' and Herod the Great's good friend. There were many Roman Judaeans with the *nomen* (Roman hereditary clan-/surname) Julius, whose families had been sponsored by Gaius Julius Caesar and Caesar Augustus (Stein 1992, 144-45). But what is significant here is that the weight informs us as to the date that Agrippa was *not agoronomos*, meaning he would have held this job immediately before or after this time. Interestingly, Sejanus was arrested and executed in AD 31, after Antonia Minor had informed Tiberius of the prefect's conspiracy (Josephus, 18.181-2). This information is only related by Josephus, who was a relative of Agrippa I and had some connection with Agrippa I's son, Agrippa II. This would infer that Antonia's agent who had informed her on Sejanus' involvement was none other than Agrippa I (Kokkinos 1998, 274). Agrippa had been Drusus' very close or even closest friend: he would have been in a good position to access incriminating information leading him to suspect that Sejanus had murdered Drusus, and he was close to the influential Antonia Minor (Josephus, 18.143-6).

Sejanus had had reason to murder Drusus. He would have feared Drusus' achieving the Principate: Drusus had resented the ambitious Sejanus' influence over his father, Tiberius, to the point that the two had quarrelled and Drusus had struck Sejanus (Tacitus, *Annals* IV.3). It would now have been dangerous for Sejanus had Drusus become Caesar (Shaw 1990, 284- 87). Sejanus had little hope of become Caesar himself, and the sources do not make logical sense in implicating Julia Livilla, Drusus' wife and Antonia's daughter, in Drusus' assassination (Tacitus, *Annals* IV.3), since Sejanus would have been a poor political substitute as her spouse for Tiberius' heir apparent. Sejanus was not patrician but of the lower equestrian class. However, Livilla's young sons were Tiberius' heirs following Drusus' death, and the enterprising Sejanus could have hoped to become the power behind the next young Caesar's throne by marrying Livilla and offering himself as her children's protector and regent (Shaw 1990, 284-87). He attempted to do just that by asking Tiberius for the widowed Livilla's hand (Tacitus, *Annals*, IV.39). Sejanus would have known that Agrippa had been sufficiently close to Drusus to have had access to information and/or to have observed details which implicated Sejanus in Drusus' death: details which Agrippa then related to his patroness, Antonia. However, Agrippa was prevented from approaching Tiberius for help with his career, and it would seem justifiable according to this line of reasoning that Sejanus would not have wished Agrippa to attain access to the Princeps due to his concerns about Agrippa's knowledge, and, therefore, barred Agrippa from Tiberius' presence. By this argument, Agrippa not only exhausted his inheritance, as Josephus states (Josephus, 18.143- 6), but also felt unsafe from Sejanus, so he returned to *Judaea*, to the area of the *Malhata* fortress, to lie low until Antonia felt ready to approach Tiberius with her intelligence. The sensitivity of this information and the risk entailed in accusing Sejanus would be the reason for the long delay.

In any event, Agrippa returned to Rome from *Syria* and *Judaea* (Josephus, 18.151-67) in AD 32 to 34, a little after Sejanus' death in AD 31. It would also make sense, according to this argument, that he worked for Antipas just after AD 31, rather than before it. Antipas the tetrarch had been a friend of Sejanus (Josephus, 18.245-56; Legge 2021), so it was safe now for Agrippa to come out of hiding at *Malatha* and work for his uncle. He also needed to gain intelligence on political events in *Judaea* so as to improve his own career prospects. Therefore, he found employment with Antipas where he could learn of his uncle the tetrarch's underhand dealings with *Parthia* and other activities (Josephus, 18.245-56), fleeing afterwards (when Antipas came to suspect him and the situation became unsafe) to his old Roman friend, Flaccus, now the Syrian governor stationed in Antioch (Josephus, 18.147-60), for employment and protection. When he was ready with his new information, he quickly returned to Italy (Kokkinos 1998, 278), and Antonia paid him. Tiberius no longer refused to meet Agrippa and welcomed him back (Josephus, 18.161-67) since, according to this line of argument, Tiberius would have now known that Agrippa had been Antonia Minor's informer.

However, if Agrippa had needed to hide, why would he have stayed at or near a fortress connected with a caravanserai, in a strategic position at a Palestinian crossroads on the Frankincense Trail? In fact, archaeological evidence for Tel *Malhata* confirms that the fortress was abandoned during the period that Agrippa was there, although it would have remained a good location for him to access main roads for information and basic supplies, and also to lie low, perhaps passing as a middle-class local on an obscure little farming property. We shall now discuss *Malhata* from the archaeological viewpoint, including the stratigraphic evidence for the site's temporary abandonment. Understanding something of *Malhata* and its situation in the early first century AD from the material record helps support the historical details and better understand the circumstances involving our hero, Agrippa.

The Topography of Malhata

Geographically, Tel *Malhata* is in a 48-km.-wide region in the *Nahal* Beersheva valley in the southern Judaean Negev (Roman *Idumaea*, or the land of the Edomites) near Hebron. A tel is a mound or hill formed by the accumulation over many centuries or millennia of archaeological strata. In Arabic, *Malhata* is known as Tel *el-Milh* ('hill of salt', possibly referring to salt production from the nearby Dead Sea, although no archaeological evidence for this has been found at the tel to date) (Beit-Arieh 2015, 11). The region is mostly composed of white and red limestone. The valley base is fertile since it is filled with loess from silt and clay, although rainfall varies in different areas of the region. The northern limit of this area is the southern sector of the Central Judaean Highlands. The Highlands form a plateau at their highest altitude near Hebron; this plateau reaches *Beni Na'im* at its southwest at 951 m., and *Khirbet Qaryatain* at its southeast at 912 m. The mountain ridge descends via three spurs on its way to *Nahal* Beersheva: it extends from *Ben Na'im* to Beersheva, and from Dura to Tel *Malhata* at 369 m. and then circles Tel *Arad* to reach the Negev Highlands at *Ras ez-Zuweira*. The southern portion of Tel *Malhata* is also called *Harei Ira*. The spurs are 10 to 15 km. wide to the north but become narrower going southwards. Therefore, *Malhata* is located in a fertile Negev basin surrounded by mountains (Pazout 2015, 11-13).

Thus, Tel *Malhata*, at the centre of the *Nahal* Beersheva valley, is on the left slopes of *Nahal Malhata*, near where the wadis of *Nahal Malhata* and *Nahal* Beersheva join. A wadi is a normally dried-up stream bed, typically only filled with water during the rainy season. A *nahal* is a mountain passage. Tel *Malhata* is at the southernmost boundaries of Roman *Judaea* (Beit-Arieh 2015, 11; Pazout 2015, 49), and is around 398 m. above sea level, making it about 10 m. higher than the surrounding land. Since it is near the level of the wadi bed, it can easily access the underground water table, and several wells have been found in the region (Pazout 2015, 49). Part of its importance is due to its location near an essential water source.

From the early twentieth century onwards, there has been much discussion as to the date of the Roman *limes* (a regularised series of frontier fortresses) there and as to whether this group of frontier defensive structures constituted a *limes* throughout the Roman period. Albrecht Alt in the 1930s suggested the *limes* dated from before the First Jewish Revolt (AD 66 to 73), while Gichon (1967, qtd. in Pazout 2015, 12-13) proposed they began during the reign of Herod I (the Great), although most scholars now believe the formalised *limes* originated during the reign of Vespasian or Diocletian, at the time of or immediately following the First Revolt. The excavation report on Tel *Malhata* published by Beit-Arieh and Freud (1998, qtd. in Pazout 2015, 13) also indicates a later fortification date (Pazout 2015, 11-13). This means that the *Malhata* fortress was not part of an organised *limes* during the earlier period that Agrippa was there, which was in the early first century AD. Organised *limes* would be required in an area that needed greater military protection from a system with centralised control. Scholars suggest this was not a requirement before the First Revolt (Pazout 2015, 11-15). In the later period just prior to and following the Revolt, desert pillaging and banditry became common in the areas bordering on *Nabataea*, but was not a serious problem in the southern frontier regions during the earlier period (Pazout,2015, 87) when *Malhata* was abandoned and Agrippa was living there.

Malhata's Strategic Importance

AS WELL AS BEING NEAR an important water source in an arid region, *Malhata* is located at a strategic position. It is 8.5 km. northeast of *Aroer*, 4.2 km. southeast of Tel *Ira* and 11.9 km. southwest of Tel *Arad*, and its central location lies upon a crossroads. One road extends north to the heart of Judaea from the Negev, and a portion of the original paved Roman road has been found 2.5 km. to the south. The east-west route connects the Dead Sea to the Mediterranean (Pazout 2015, 49). Since the site was at a junction in the centre of the *Nahal* Beersheva valley, most ancient travel routes began near the fortress, and all travellers passed through this site. The remains of the Roman road are only 300 m. to the east of the digitally-modelled 'least-cost' ideal route (Pazout 2015, 87) (a calculation based upon levelling the hilly landscape to find the optimal travel route through the area). This calculated ideal location is, according to Pazout, an impressive indication of Roman analytical ability. Travelling through the hills, the Roman roads here tend to follow passes and ridges. Many ancient travel routes and tracks were created and utilised by Bedouin groups. Roman roads were built by the military and the Judaean roads served a military patrol purpose; rabbinical writings from the second century onwards speak of Roman military patrols crossing the wilderness areas. Josephus also writes of decurions and centurions supervising security in local villages and cities. Pazout suggests that the forts in the more populated agricultural northwest portion of the Roman Negev region, being located close to roads, controlled road traffic and civilian populations, fulfilling a road policing purpose. Although there was concern about rebellion from local populations during and immediately after the Jewish Revolts, there seems to have been less need for high security during the early first century AD, so a *limes* would not have been needed at that time (Pazout 2015, 87).

Fortresses such as *Malhata*, as well as *Arad*, *Uza*, *Beersheva* and *Aroer*, in the southeasterly region between the agricultural estates and scattered herding groups, were more concerned with local safety situations involving nomadic desert tribes, and in protecting wells, water supplies and main caravan route intersections. Pazout suggests that *Malhata's* main duties would have been policing the roads of this region against brigands, acting as a road station for caravanserai, and collecting road tolls and duties; the focus was, thus, economic and trade-related rather than military. The *Malhata* fortress could easily survey the surrounding region and roads from its higher position, but the region was sparsely and transiently populated. This scattered population during Agrippa's fugitive days would have made it a good place to lie low and not draw attention to himself while he decided on his next move. The relative safety of the area during this period would seem suitable for Agrippa and his wife Cypros to stay, protected perhaps by a few servants and bodyguards. While *Malhata* and similar fortresses in the southeast Negev were able to overlook their general vicinity and immediately neighbouring forts, they were not sufficiently elevated to view areas further afield. This means they were oriented inward rather than outward, underlining their local policing purpose in areas of minimal threat, where it was only necessary to send simple messages between the forts (Pazout 2015, 87).

Figure 5 shows the relative positions and placement densities of the Negev Roman forts. It also allows one to compare the relative placement densities of the northwestern (NW) versus

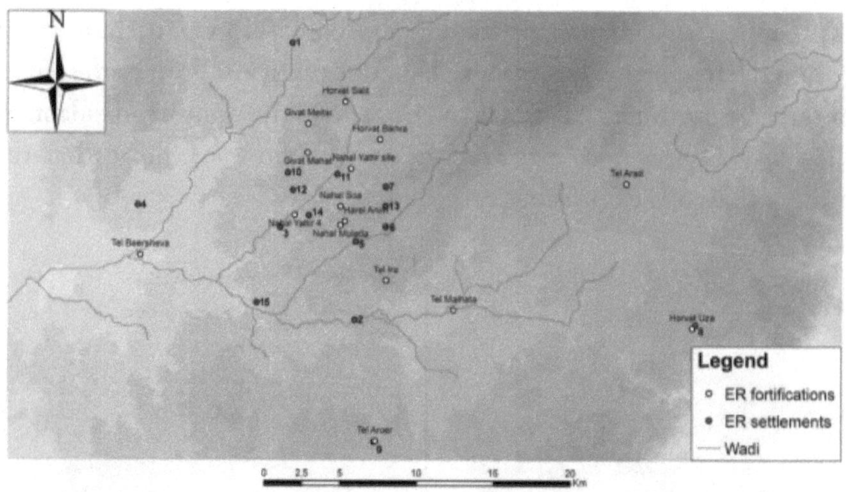

Figure 5. Map of Negev Roman fortress sites showing their relative placement density (Pazout A. 2018, 175, Fig.
2.; courtesy of the author)

SOUTHEASTERN (SE) FACETS of the area: fortresses are more densely placed in the NW than the SE sector of which *Malhata* is central, implying that fewer of them were needed in this latter (SE) region due to its relatively lower and more scattered and transient population. In the SE facet, *Malhata* occupies the intersection of major watercourses, while the other SE fortresses are not located near significant water sources. This demonstrates *Malhata*'s significance for travel routes through the area.

The succeeding visibility maps in Figure 6 also show us the relative visibilities of the NW and SE portions of the fortress group studied: The map on the left provides a close-up view of the densest sector of the NW Negev fortress group where closer policing was required due to the area's relatively higher population. The right-side map allows one to focus on the SE portion of the fortress group which occupied an area of less dense and more scattered population mostly utilised by a minority of travelling Bedouin herders and through which caravans passed. As mentioned above, this area was relatively safe from border disputes due to its importance as part of the Frankincense Trail from Arabia, so it required less policing during Herodian times until just prior to the outset of the First Revolt in AD 66. It can be seen, in the right-hand-side map, that *Malhata* occupies not only the hub of the watercourses but the centre of this SE region's fortress group.

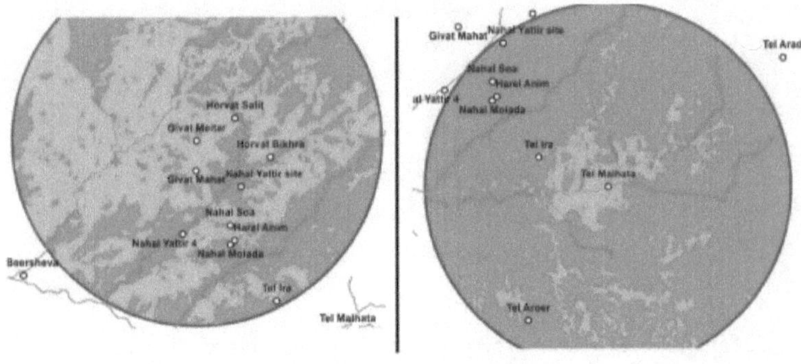

Figure 6. Negev Roman border road system reconstructed showing relative visibilities of fortress sites (Pazout, A. 2018, p. 175, Fig. 6.; courtesy of the author)

It is interesting that *Malhata*, a fort on a crossroads of main travel routes, was abandoned during this transitional period beginning during the late Hasmonaean to earlier Herodian eras and continuing until the latter half of the first century AD. Beit-Arieh *et al.* suggest the changing political climate occurring in the period between the two dynasties was the reason for the abandonment of the nearby settlement and fortress. This period of transition took place when *Judaea*'s rule by its last ethnically Jewish dynasty, the Hasmonaeans/Maccabees, ended and was replaced by the Romanised Herods after Rome made Herod I client king of *Judaea* and had him attain his kingdom militaristically. The Maccabees had ousted the Macedonian Seleucids from Judaean rule, but during the period between the Hasmonaean/Maccabee and Herodian dynasties, before Herod I established control for Rome, there was a temporary hiatus in stable governmental control. Beit-Arieh *et al.* suggest that some external Seleucid political influences during this period of unrest might have been responsible for the site's initial abandonment. They also note that the neighbouring sites of Tel Beersheva and *Horvat 'Uza* were deserted during the same period and suggest that this was for the same political reason (Beit-Arieh *et al.* 2015, 742-43*)*. The Seleucids were the Hellenistic rulers of Syria before the Romans replaced them. *Malhata* apparently continued to be abandoned, perhaps due to the mentioned lack of necessity, until the Revolt. This would have brought about a situation in which, since the area was now sparsely inhabited, Agrippa was able to make his temporary home either in the abandoned fortress or, as previously suggested, some old nearby family property he knew of from family records which had either been abandoned as well or was in the care of a local family custodian.

The Roman Judaean Negev was part of a shared economic trade route, the Frankincense Trail, between Arabia and the Mediterranean: and of much interest to both *Nabataea* and Roman *Judaea*. Cooperation between the Nabataean and Roman powers was important in the area, diminishing the potential for pillage (Pazout 2015, 92). This does not, however, rule out the possibility for banditry on a trading crossroads, but the need for a permanent fort at this time was seemingly relatively low. Since the region was remote with a focus on local, decentralised security, it would have been a good place for Agrippa to have remained hidden from the central governments of both *Judaea* and Rome. He might also have felt safer due to proximity with nearby caravan routes and patrols and could have represented himself with the help of Idumaean connections as an unimportant, small-scale land owner. Had he stayed on an old family farmstead in the region, he would have been free from close observation by policing forces, and even more so had he chosen to blend in with the sparse population of the area. Due to his propensity for intrigue, we might speculate on local activities he became involved in before he and his wife were finally able to move to Tiberias. It is certainly interesting to consider the balance required between lying low, away from Imperial notice, and needing to stay in a remote, unfamiliar desert area with a culture very different from the elite Roman one to which he was accustomed.

Malhata's Archaeological Remains

TOPOGRAPHICALLY, THE *Malhata's* tel is on a flat, oval, natural platform that rises a few metres above the wadi bed, measuring 190 x 95 m. It spans two levels: an upper eastern one taking up 25% of the tel and the lower western one covering the rest of the mound. Archaeological surveys demonstrated that the upper area had been occupied by a Roman fortified camp of ca. 3.75 dunams with a 2 m. stone wall which dated from the Roman period or a little earlier in the Hellenistic era (Beit-Arieh 2015, 11-15).

Even before excavation began, the fortress' outline could be seen. Following excavation, the partially unearthed fortress building is found to be rectangular and to measure 75 x 55 m. Its walls are wider than 1 m.; the fortress has outworks and towers and can easily observe and control its surroundings due to its higher location. These combined features help in its clear identification as a fortress, but, as already noted, it is not highly visible beyond its general vicinity since its elevation is still relatively low and is hidden by some of its surrounding terrain. Since limited excavation has been achieved on the structure to-date, its internal plan is still not well known. Two long rooms have been identified on the east side, and five casemates along its northern walls, with eight more on its west and another five at its south. At least two of these are paved with stone blocks. The *enceinte*, or enclosure wall, is 1.25 m. wide and was made from cut ashlar blocks with the spaces between them filled with small stones (Pazout 2015). However, the casemates date mostly to the Middle Bronze and Iron Ages and are in Area B and Section W in the north and Area C in the west (Tal 2015b, 19-20).

As mentioned previously, the site contains some of the few water sources found in the entire region, which also contributes toward its importance. Good wells were found at the foot of the eastern portion of the tel. Because of this, the location has often, until recently, been used by large Bedouin groups raising sheep and goats. These groups have worked the land and buried their dead in the vicinity, as seen in the archaeological record. In fact, numerous Bedouin burials have intruded into different archaeological strata, causing much information to be lost from earlier eras. It is possible that the ancient settlement's connection with salt means it was a trading post for *Gebel Sodom*, important for its salt production (Beit-Arieh 2015, 11-15).

The Tel's Stratigraphy

STRATIGRAPHY REFERS to a location's strata or levels, each of which occupies diverse, successive dating periods. The *Malhata* site's earliest strata, VI-III, date to the Bronze and Iron Ages. However, the Hellenistic to Roman period of interest to this article occupies Strata II to I (Beit- Arieh 2015, 11-15; Freud 2015, 118-120). There is a smaller tel, known as Small Tel *Malhata,* on a low, flat ridge on the northern bank of Wadi Malhata, which was mainly occupied in the Chalcolithic and Early Bronze Ages, and south and east of the main tel are a few large Roman and Byzantine sites (Beit-Arieh 2015, 15-16). West of the fortress, in Area G, are several more Roman structures of unclear purpose (Pazout 2015, 50).

Two of *Malhata*'s strata are Hellenistic (third to second centuries BC) and Late Roman (second, third, and fourth centuries AD), respectively. Later excavations have revealed that the site was also active in the Early Roman period from the late first to second centuries AD. However, the pottery sherds found there date to the first half of the first century BC, and the few coins uncovered date to the time of the last Hasmonaean kings, John Hyrcanus or Alexander Jannaeus (Pazout 2015,

50, 62, 80-81), which indicates that the site was abandoned in the first century BC.

Types of Material Remains

Coinage

HELLENISTIC REMAINS at the site (second to early first centuries BC) are scant and are found in Areas B and C and Section W. They seem to indicate that the site was a Hellenistic fortress before it became a Roman one, since they occupy the same terrain as the later Roman fortress and Iron Age military fortifications. For example, the Hellenistic wall of 22 K. is directly below Roman fortress Wall 2. The limited Hellenistic potsherds found belong, in particular, to Eastern *Sigillata* A (ESA) from the first century BC, suggesting a Hasmonaean connection. The coins found associated with this pottery belong to Antiochus IV and VII, but also include the two Hasmonaean coins mentioned. Since there is no evidence for the site being destroyed during this time, it is believed it was simply abandoned during the time of John Hyrcanus or King Alexander Jannaeus (who reigned from 103 to 76 BC), perhaps during or before the time of Antipater I, the advisor to Alexander Jannaeus and father of Herod I and of the Romanised client-king Herodian Dynasty (Josephus, 14; Beit-Arieh 2015, 17-18; Beit-Arieh et al. 2015, 742-43). 50 bronze coins have been uncovered from the second century BC to the fifth century AD in the Byzantine era. Alexander Jannaeus' coins are plentiful in Hasmonaean/Maccabean sites, but are completely absent from this one, which also suggests that its occupation was interrupted beginning in the first century BC. Four coins were discovered in the Roman strata of Area B, six in the refuse piles and surface of this region and three in the Area C refuse dump. All other coins were discovered on the surface. Most coins were not well preserved, and only a few of them can be attributed to a particular ruler (Kindler 2015, 684). The coin findings list, adapted from Kindler (ibid.), is presented in Table 1.

Table 1. (Adapted from Kindler, A. Hellenistic, Roman and Byzantine Coins. In: Beit-Arieh, I. and Freud, L. *Tel Malhata: A Central City in the Biblical Negev*

(Monograph Series of the Institute of Archaeology of Tel Aviv University 32). Tel Aviv and Winona Lake, 2015, Fig. 16.1; courtesy of the Institute of Archaeology of Tel Aviv University).

Reg. number	Number of Coins	Area	Identification
Seleucid Coins			
268/60	1	B	Antiochus IV Epiphanes (175-164 BCE)
490/60	1	C Surface	Antiochus VII (138-129 BCE)
Hasmonaean Coins			
493/60	2	Surface	John Hyrcanus I (129-104 BCE)
496/60			
Roman City Coins			
302/60	1	B Surface	Caesarea Maritima (ca. 250 CE)
367/60, 247/60	5	B Surface	Unidentified
490/61-62, 403/60		C Surface	Suggested as Third Century

FIGURE 7 PRESENTS IMAGES of the few coins found at *Malhata* dating to the late Seleucid and late Hasmonaean period. Only one Roman coin could be definitely identified: this is a coin from Caesarea produced c.AD 250 under Trajanus Decius or Trebonianus Gallus. From that time onwards, coin remains become more continuous, all being minted during the reigns of the Caesars from the second half of the third

Century AD. Following this period, coins are also found from the fourth and fifth centuries AD (Kindler, 2015, 684).

Figure 7. (Kindler, A. Hellenistic, Roman and Byzantine Coins. In: Beit-Arieh, I. and Freud, L. *Tel Malhata: A Central City in the Biblical Negev* (Monograph Series of the Institute of Archaeology of Tel Aviv University 32). Tel Aviv and Winona Lake, 2015, Fig. 16.1, Nos. 1-4; courtesy of the Institute of Archaeology of Tel Aviv University)

Description of the coins

DESCRIPTION OF THE COINS[3]

No. 1 (Fig. 16.1: 1)
Reg. No. 268/60 Locus 417, Area B
Antiochus IV Epiphanes
Date: 173–168 BCE
Mint: Ake-Ptolemais(?)
Diameter: 13–14 mm
Weight: 1.98 gr
Obverse: Head of Antiochus IV right, diademed and radiate
Reverse: Veiled and draped goddess standing enface, holding long scepter or torch; obliterated legend

No. 2 (Fig. 16.1: 2)
Reg. No. 490/60 Area C (dump)
Antiochus VII
Date: 138–129 BCE
Mint: Antioch
Diameter: 18.0–18.5 mm
Weight: 6.11 gr
Obverse: Bust of Eros right
Reverse: Isis headdress, across field: ΒΑΣΙΛΕΩΣ ΑΝΤΙΟΧΟΥ-ΕΥΕΡΓΕΤΟΥ; date obliterated

No. 3 (Fig. 16.1: 3)
Reg. No. 493/60, surface (eastern foothill of the tell)
Hasmonean, John Hyrcanus I (?)
Date: 129–104 BCE(?)
Mint: Jerusalem
Diameter: 12–13.5 mm
Weight: 1.70 gr

No. 4 (Fig. 16.1: 4)
Reg. No. 496/60 surface (outside the tell)
Hasmonean, John Hyrcanus I(?)
Date: 129–104 BCE(?)
Mint: Jerusalem
Diameter: 13.0–13.5 mm
Weight: 2.06 gr
Obverse: Double cornucopia with pomegranate between horns
Reverse: Obliterated legend in wreath

Architectural Remains Roman and Byzantine Phases

IN ADDITION TO ITS by Josephus, another historical record on Malatha is the *Notitia Dignitatum Orientis* XXXII (*Dux Palaestinae*), which refers to the presence of the 45 '*Cohors Prima Flauia, Moleatha*'. This account dates to c. AD 411-413 during the Roman-to-Byzantine era. From this, we know that the fortress was then garrisoned by the *Cohors I Flavia*. Earlier records from *Syria* speak of the *Palaestina* Bar Kokhba Revolt in the 130s AD and state that this cohort was then present in the region (Russel 1995). It is suggested that the non-military settlement whose remains are found near the fortress may have been occupied by the soldiers' families, since these troops were *limitanei* (frontier soldiers). Thus, except for some sparse potsherd finds which provide evidence for sporadic habitation, the site was abandoned during the time that Josephus (18.147-50) mentions Agrippa I's hiding in a 'tower' there, which would have been in the 20s to early 30s AD. This period of abandonment again supports the theory that this was Josephus' Malatha, meeting Agrippa's need to hide during that period in a well-connected area with good access to water sources, provisions and communication routes.

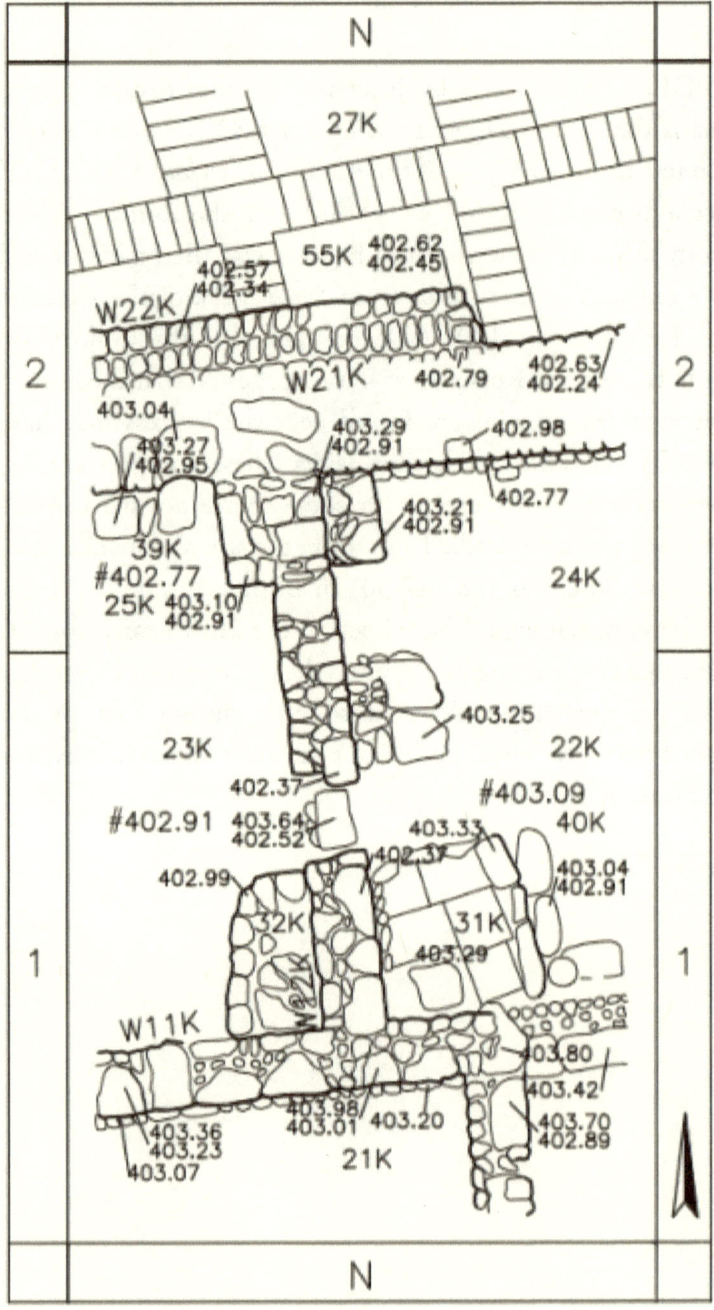

N
27K
55K
402.62
402.45
402.57
402.34
W22K
2
W21K
402.79
402.63
402.24
403.04
403.29
402.91
402.98
403.27
402.95
402.77
403.21
402.91
39K
#402.77
24K
25K 403.10
402.91
403.25
23K
22K
402.37
#403.09
#402.91
403.64
402.52
40K
403.33
402.37
403.04
402.91
402.99
32K
31K
403.29
W11K
403.80
403.42
403.98
403.01
403.20
403.70
402.89
403.36
403.23
403.07
21K
N
2
1
1

Figure 8. Sketch of part of Roman building in Section W, Tel *Malhata* (Freud,

L. The First Expedition: Sections W and Z. In: Beit-Arieh, I. and Freud, L. *Tel Malhata: A Central City in the Biblical Negev* (Monograph Series of the Institute of Archaeology of Tel Aviv University 32). Tel Aviv and Winona Lake, 2015, Figs. 2.115; courtesy of the Institute of Archaeology of Tel Aviv University).

IN TERMS OF THE FORTRESS' Roman and Byzantine phases of occupation, the floor of the Late Roman structure matches that of the earlier building phase prior to its abandonment and no renovation can be observed to its outer walls, which further substantiates the surmise that the Roman phase begins in the late first century AD. The site was abandoned again in the late second to early third centuries AD, so its habitation phase is the same as that of the *Hovat Uzah* and Tel Beersheva fortresses. Area G contains several Roman structures of unknown use (Pazout 2015, 50). Beit-Arieh and Freud's expedition publication has identified the structures shown in Figures 8 to 16 as belonging to the Roman architectural phase.

Pottery Remains

POTTERY ASSEMBLAGES from the Hellenistic era are scant, which further supports abandonment of the site until the latter half of the first century AD (Beit-Arieh et al. 2015, 742-43). Beit-Arieh and Freud's expedition publication dates the architecture in Areas B and C to two Roman and Byzantine phases, Strata IB and IA. The similarly scant Roman pottery sherds found are dated to two groups: Early to Middle Roman of the first, second and early third centuries AD and Late Roman to Early Byzantine of the fourth to fifth centuries AD (Tal, 2015b, 19-20).

Figure 9. Image of fortress wall, Tel *Malhata* (Freud, L. The First Expedition: Sections W and Z. In: Beit-Arieh, I. and Freud, L. *Tel Malhata: A Central City in the Biblical Negev* (Monograph Series of the Institute of Archaeology of Tel Aviv University 32). Tel Aviv and Winona Lake, 2015, Figs. 2.116; courtesy of the Institute of Archaeology of Tel Aviv University).

(Monograph Series of the Institute of Archaeology of Tel Aviv University 32). Tel Aviv and Winona Lake, 2015, Figs. 2.117-122; courtesy of the Institute of Archaeology of Tel Aviv University).

Figure 10, left and Figure 11, right. Images of areas below the fortress wall, Tel *Malhata* Both from (Freud, L. The First Expedition: Sections W and Z. In: Beit-Arieh, I. and Freud, L. *Tel Malhata: A Central City in the Biblical Negev* (Monograph Series of the Institute of Archaeology of Tel Aviv University 32). Tel Aviv and Winona Lake, 2015, Figs. 2.122; courtesy of the Institute of Archaeology of Tel Aviv University).

Figure 12. Area below part of wall, Tel *Malhata* (Freud, L. The First Expedition: Sections W and Z. In: Beit-Arieh, I. and Freud, L. *Tel Malhata: A Central City in the Biblical Negev*

Figure 13 above, Figure 14 below. Areas below the fortress walls. (Freud, L. The First Expedition: Sections W and Z. In: Beit-Arieh, I. and Freud, L. *Tel Malhata: A Central City in the Biblical Negev* (Monograph Series of the Institute of Archaeology of Tel Aviv University 32). Tel Aviv and Winona Lake, 2015, Figs. 2.118; courtesy of the Institute of Archaeology of Tel Aviv University).

Figure 15 above and Figure 16 below. Area below the fortress wall. (Freud, L. The First Expedition: Sections W and Z. In: Beit-Arieh, I. and Freud, L. *Tel Malhata: A Central City in the Biblical Negev* (Monograph Series of the Institute of Archaeology of Tel Aviv University 32). Tel Aviv and Winona Lake, 2015, Figs. 2.118; courtesy of the Institute of Archaeology of Tel Aviv University).

Glass and Metal Material Findings

OTHER TYPES OF ARCHAEOLOGICAL material are also found in the Roman phases of the Tel *Malhata* fortress. Twelve fragmentary glass vessels were uncovered in Areas A, B, D and G, either on Roman floors which date to the Early and Late Roman periods, or in fills dating to the Byzantine era. Other such vessels were either on the surfaces or intruding into the Iron Age strata. These finds all date from the late first century AD and later. Thus, these remains again support the hypothesis that the site had been abandoned until the second half of the first century AD. The objects are typical of domestic vessels used throughout

Palestine at the time, and were probably used by the fortress inhabitants (Tal 2015a, 691, 695).

Scattered assemblages of metal objects dating to the Hellenistic, Roman and Byzantine periods are made from iron and bronze, and include brass items and weaponry. Most metal objects were used for structural fittings, including nails. The majority of the metal items from these periods were found in Strata B, C and W (Tal 2015a, 698) and are listed in Table 2.

Early Roman glass vessels were found on the 'lower Roman floor' of Area B but these date to the late first century AD and intrude into an Iron Age stratum of Area A. Glass finds are sparse and consist of daily use tableware including beakers, bowls and lamp-bowls apparently used by the fortress inhabitants when the fort was occupied (Jackson-Tal 2015, 691 & 695). Glass vessels from the early Roman period, found at Tel *Malhata*, are as Figure 17.

Figure 17. Tel *Malhata* glass assemblage sketches, early Roman (late first century AD) (Jackson-Tal, R.E. Glass Vessels. In: Beit-Arieh, I. and Freud, L. *Tel Malhata: A Central City in the Biblical Negev* (Monograph Series of the Institute of Archaeology of Tel Aviv University 32). Tel Aviv and Winona Lake, 2015, Fig. 17.1; courtesy of the Institute of Archaeology of Tel Aviv University).

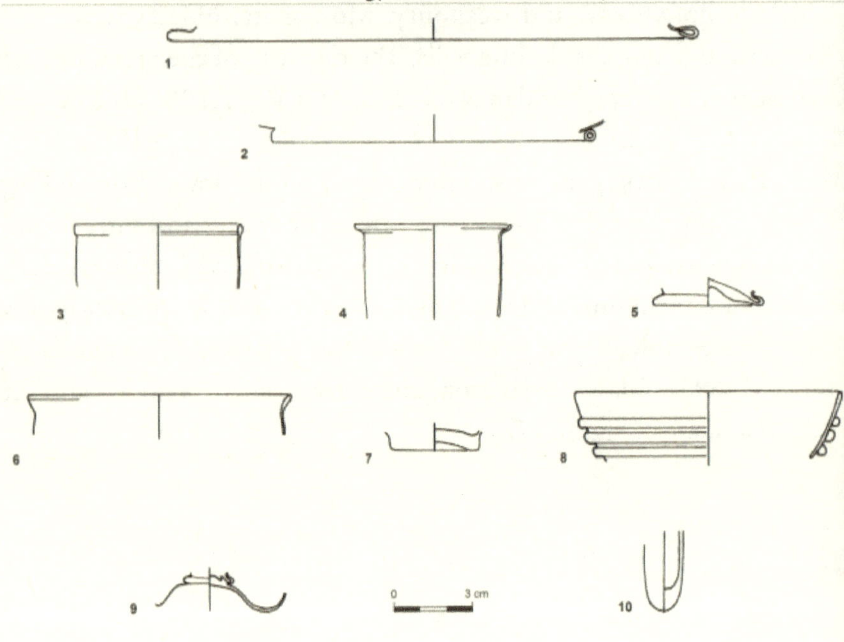

Table 2. List of metal assemblages from Strata B, C and W in Tel *Malhata*, dating to the Hellenistic, Roman and Byzantine periods (Tal, O. Metal Objects. In: Beit-Arieh, I. and Freud, L. *Tel Malhata: A Central City in the Biblical Negev* (Monograph Series of the Institute of Archaeology of Tel Aviv University 32). Tel Aviv and Winona Lake, 2015, pp. 699-700; courtesy of the Institute of Archaeology of Tel Aviv University).

No.	Type	Locus no.	Reg. No.	Elevation	Area	Stratum	Material	Measurements (cm)	Weight (g)	Fig.	Comments
1	Spearhead (fragment)	453	815/60	3.98	B	II	Iron	L. 6	13	18.1.1: 1	Tang is missing
2	Nail	437	356/61	3.53	B	II	Iron	L. 4.9, head D. 2.2	14	18.1.1: 2	
3	Nail	627	489/60	4.51	C	II	Iron	L. 6.3, head D. 1.8; L. 2.4	20	18.1.1: 3	Two parts of the same nail
4	Bracelet (fragment)	603	408/60	2.69	C	Mixed	Iron	L. 6.5	11	18.1.1: 4	Pointed end is intact
5	Nail (fragment)	419	305/60	2.93	B	IB	Iron	L. 5	9	18.1.1: 5	Curved, head is missing
6	Sheet (hoe/ shovel?)	437	356/60	3.53	B	II	Iron	L. 11, W. 7, T. 0.4	86	18.1.1: 6	
7	Cosmetic spoon	31K	137/1/60	402.80	W	II	Bronze			18.1.1: 7	
8	Pin	Surface	495/60		C	I?	Bronze	L. 9.2		18.1.1: 8	
9	Fibula (fragment)	402	220/60	2.4	B	IA	Bronze	L. 3.1	1	18.1.1: 9	Flattened edge
10	Fibula (fragment)	614	439/60	2.5	C	II	Bronze	D. 3.3	2	18.1.1: 10	Flattened edge has a flattened metal piece attached
11	Bowl/libation vessel (*patera*)	Surface	492/60	-		I?	Bronze	L. 6.5, D. 4, H. 15	37	18.1.1: 11	
12	Nail (fragment)	401	206/60	2.42	B	I	Bronze	L. 3			
13	Nail (fragment)	403	225/60	2.31	B	IA	Iron	L. 2.4, W. 1.2	2		
14	Bead	403	213/60	2.25	B	I	Bronze	L. 1.5, W. 0.7	3		
15	Nail (fragment)	419	305/61	2.93	B	I	Iron	L. 5.5	10		Head is missing
16	Nail	429	379/60	3.05	B	IB	Iron	L. 2, head D. 1.1	2		
17	Bracelet	429	282/60	2.72	B	IB	Bronze	D. 5			
18	Nail (fragment)	433	310/60	3.41	B	IB	Bronze	L. 1.5			
19	Ring	452	398/60	4.02	B	II	Bronze	D. 0.5			
20	Nail (fragment)	601	407/60	3.68	C	I	Bronze				
21	Nail (fragment)	604	418/60	3.09-3.99	C	I	Iron				Large number specimens
22	Bracelet	604	416/60	3.69-3.99	C	I	Bronze	D. 5			
23	Hook	622	474/60	4.2	C	II	Iron	L. 10.5	15		
24	Nail (fragment)	622	464/60	4.05	C	II	Iron		7		
25	Ring	Surface	495/61		C	I?	Bronze	D. 3			
26	Ring	Surface	495/62		C	I?	Bronze	D. 2			
27	Bracelet	Surface	495/63		C	I?	Bronze	D. 4			
28	Nail (fragment)	Surface	495/64		C	I?	Bronze	L. 3.5			Curved at tip

No.	Type	Locus no.	Reg. No.	Elevation	Area	Stratum	Material	Measure-ments (cm)	Weight (g)	Fig.	Comments
29	Tongue (of a bell)	Surface	495/65		C	I?	Bronze	L. 1.1			
30	Cosmetic spoon (fragment)	Surface	495/66		C	I?	Bronze	D. 1			
31	Nails (fragments)	Surface	492/60		C	I?	Iron				Large number specimens
32	Nail	Surface	491/60		C	I?	Iron	L. 10			
33	Nail	24k	126/60	402.8-402.57	W	II	Iron	L. 4, head D. 2, W. 0.8			

Conclusion

Based on the archaeological excavations conducted so far on Tel *Malhata*, the site appears to have been abandoned from the late first century BC to the late first century AD, although there was probably some continued policing of the roads by Roman patrols, due to the overall area's importance to the Frankincense Trail and the presence of wells in that semi-arid region. *Malhata's* environs were a good source of water, and this would have attracted its use by Bedouin groups. *Malhata* fortress was on a strategic and economically significant Roman crossroads for travel between the Negev and the main part of *Judaea*, and between the Mediterranean and Dead Seas. Part of a Roman road forming a portion of this network has been revealed near *Malhata*. We could hypothesise that Herod I's very Roman grandson, Agrippa, had rural ancestral holdings in the area where he was able to lie low during his fugitive period, although he may potentially also have hidden at least for part of the time in the abandoned fortress itself. Josephus' mention of a 'tower' makes the exact location of his hiding place unclear. The drastic and sudden change of lifestyle for Agrippa, from being an adopted member of the Julio-Claudian family living in Rome to a poverty-stricken fugitive and private citizen hiding in a remote semi-desert region, must have been traumatic, which would explain why Josephus relates that Agrippa nearly committed suicide while he was there (18.147-50). It is also to be noted that suicide would have been in contradiction to Jewish Law (e.g. *Genesis* 9.5), but was acceptable and honourable behaviour for a Roman in a time of crisis and lost status, which indicates the degree of Agrippa's Roman self-identify, at least at this point in his life. He had, after all, grown up in Rome among the Julio-Claudian children from the age of five or younger (Josephus, 18.143-46).

Postscript

What became of Agrippa I subsequent to this period?

Following his return to Italy, Agrippa I was welcomed back by Antonia Minor and Caesar Tiberius and given a position with Tiberius on Capri. With the help of both his friends, the Caesars Gaius Caligula and Claudius, he achieved his kingdom of Judaea and praetorian and consular decorations, and his final kingdom covered a greater territory than that of his grandfather, Herod the Great. Due to his influence on the younger Caligula, he persuaded the Caesar to at least defer his misguided plan to place his statue as Zeus in the Jerusalem Temple, thus preventing a Jewish Revolt at that time. He also helped Claudius achieve the Principate following Caligula's assassination, and successfully negotiated with the Senate to prevent civil war (Josephus, 18, 19).

As king of Judaea, despite his own apparently liberal adherence to Judaism, he was committed to following the Jewish Laws when in Jerusalem (Josephus, 19.328), to the extent that he is mentioned frequently as having done so in the *Talmud* (BT *Kettubot*, 17a; *m. Bikkurim* 3.4; *m. Sotah*, 7; etc.). He was also apparently the only Herod allowed into Jerusalem's inner Temple precincts, whose entry by non-Jews was punishable by death (even Herod I had been unable to enter) (*m. Sotah*, 7; Kokkinos 2015, 92; Josephus, 15). There, he read the *Torah* to the attendees during an important Jewish ceremony, possibly the Feast of Tabernacles, and was publicly recognized by the Jewish leaders as not merely a Roman client king but a Jewish king. This seems partly owing to his being the grandson of Herod the Great's Jewish queen Mariamne the Hasmonaean (Maccabean) (Josephus, 18), but also due to his talent with negotiation and his charisma. He himself claimed to identify as both a Roman and a Jew (Philo. *Ad Gaium*, 25), so he seems to have been quite multicultural in his outlook.

He was comfortable living in the Roman city of Caesarea as well, and he officiated at a huge gladiatorial festival in Roman Berytus (Beirut). He seems to have had supporters among the Greco-Romans, too, and he was exuberantly acclaimed in Greek cultural fashion while leading another enormous ceremony in Caesarea. His growing popularity and ambition may have inspired the envy of the new Roman Syrian governor, Marsus. He died very suddenly shortly after being cheered while leading the Caesarean Games in honour of Rome, and his rapid symptoms together with the political climate suggest that this was not from natural causes. Numerous Jewish people throughout Judaea prayed for him as he lay dying, including outside his window, and then grieved for him following his death, and the riots that broke out immediately afterwards which were at least partly precipitated by his loss led to the First Revolt around twenty years later. Judaea had been peaceful during his rule, and there is no record of Zealot activity occurring then (Josephus, 19; *Acts* 12:19-23). It appears he had been generally attempting to offset the diverse factions and cultures in and connected with Judaea, although he tended to side with the Jews rather than the Greeks in disputes (Josephus, 19; *Acts* 12).

Although Agrippa saw himself as both a Roman and a Jew, he seems to have been very Roman in his attitude and attachment for Rome when he first fled to the Negev. He may have learned from his unpleasant experience that he could achieve much more by being loyal to not only one person, as he had been to Drusus, but to anyone in Roman power at the time. In this approach, his ability at diplomacy and intrigue resembles that of his great- grandfather Antipater I and his grandfather Herod the Great (Josephus, 13-16, etc.), although he appears to have lacked Herod's later harshness.

Agrippa seems to have seen this period of flight to the Negev as a turning point in his life, since when he first became king of Judaea, he spoke to a large gathering at the Temple of Jerusalem on how God can allow the prosperous to fall but sometimes also raises again those who have fallen (Josephus, 19.292).

Bibliography

Beit-Arieh, I. 2015: 'Tal Malhata: The Site'. In: Beit-Arieh, I. and Freud, L. *Tel Malhata: A Central City in the Biblical Negev*. Tel Aviv and Winona Lake, 2015, Chapter 1, 11-16.

Beit-Arieh, I., Freud, L., & Tal, O. 2015: 'Summary: Tel Malhata – From the Middle Bronze Age to the Byzantine Period'. In: Beit-Arieh, I. and Freud, L. *Tel Malhata: A Central City in the Biblical Negev*. Tel Aviv and Winona Lake, 2015, Chapter 22, 739-746.

Cassius Dio. 2021: *Roman History*, Reproduced from Loeb Classical Library ed., *VII*, 1924. Also available at penelope.uchicago.edu[1], 2021, accessed Feb 2023.

Curran, J. 2014, '"Philorhomaioi": The Herods between Rome and Jerusalem', *Journal for the Study of Judaism in the Persian, Hellenistic, and Roman Period*. 45(4/5), 2014, 493-522.

Flavius Josephus, 1737: William Whiston, translator, *The Genuine Words of Flavius Josephus the Jewish Historian*. Translated from the original Greek according to Havercamp's accurate edition. Also available at <penelope.uchicago.edu[2]>, accessed Feb 2023.

Fontanille, J.-P., and Kogon, A. 2018: *The Coinage of Herod Antipas: A Study and Die Classification of the Earliest Coins of Galilee*, May 1, 2018.

Freud, L. 'The First Expedition: Sections W and Z'. In: Beit-Arieh, I. and Freud, L. *Tel Malhata: A Central City in the Biblical Negev*. Tel Aviv and Winona Lake, 2015, Chapter 2, 107-140.

Jackson-Tal, R.E. 'Glass Vessels'. In: Beit-Arieh, I. and Freud, L. Tel Malhata: A Central City in the Biblical Negev. Tel Aviv and Winona Lake, 2015, Chapter 17, 691-697.

Kindler, A. 'Hellenistic, Roman and Byzantine Coins'. In: Beit-Arieh, I. and Freud, L. Tel Malhata: A Central City in the Biblical Negev. Tel Aviv and Winona Lake, 2015.

Kokkinos, N. 1998: 'The Herodian Dynasty: Origins, Role in Society and Eclipse'. *Journal of the Study of the Pseudpigrapha Supplement Series* 30. Sheffield Academic Press, 1998.

Kokkinos, Nikos *et al.*, 2015, *Aspects of Jerusalem under Herod*. Paper Archaeological, Historical and Geographical Studies, Eretz-Israel, 2015, 79-109.

Kropp, A. J. M. 2021: 'Crowning the Emperor an Unorthodox Image of Claudius, Agrippa I and Herod of Chalkis, *Syria*.' *Archeologie, Art et Histoire*. 90. 2013/2021, 377-89.

---

1.   http://penelope.uchicago.edu/

2.   http://penelope.uchicago.edu/

Legge, E. 2021: 'Marcus Julius Agrippa I: A Re-evaluation of Certain Events Taking Place in His Life'. Paper presentation, *Chartered Institute for Archaeologists Festival*, July 26, 2021.

Legge, E. 2023: *Herodian Era Toprography and Archaeology to Throw Light on the Life of Marcus Julius Agrippa I*[3]. (etd-05092023-165006) [Master's thesis, University of Pisa]. Pisa: University of Pisa, 2023.

Meyers, E. M., and Mark, A. 2012: *From Herod to the Great Revolt. Alexander to Constantine: Archaeology of the Land of the Bible*. III. Yale University Press, 2012.

Pazout, A. 2015: *Spatial Analysis of Early Roman Fortifications in Northern Negev*. Prague: Charles University of Prague: Institute of Classical Archaeology, Diploma Thesis, 2015. <https://dspace.cuni.[4] cz/handle/20.500.11956/64325[5]>, accessed Feb 2023.

Philo Judaeus, 1855, C.D. Yonge, translator, *The Works of Philo Judaeus*. Also available at <penelope.[6] uchicago.edu[7]>, accessed Feb 2023.

Schwartz, D. R.1989: *Agrippa I: The Last King of Judea*. Tubingen: JCB Mohr.

Stein, A.1992: 'Gaius Julius, an Agoronomos from Tiberias', *Zeitschrift fuer Papyrologie und Epigraphik*. 93. 1992, 144-48.

Tal, O. 'Metal Objects'. In: Beit-Arieh, I. and Freud, L. *Tel Malhata: A Central City in the Biblical Negev*. Tel Aviv and Winona Lake, 2015a, Chapter 18, 698-700.

Tal, O. 'The Hellenistic, Roman and Byzantine Settlements: Archaeological-Historical Background'. In: Beit-Arieh, I. and Freud, L. *Tel Malhata: A Central City in the Biblical Negev*. Tel Aviv and Winona Lake, 2015b, Chapter 2, 17-26.

Talmud. Sefaria. [on-line]. Available at <https://www.sefaria.org/texts/Talmud/Yerushalmi[8]>

---

3. *https://www.researchgate.net/publication/*

378140707_Herodian_Era_Toprography_and_Archaeology_to_Throw_Light_on_the_Life_of_Marcus_Julius_Agrippa

_I?_tp=eyJjb250ZXh0Ijp7ImZpcnN0UGFnZSI6InByb2ZpbGUiLCJwYWdlIjoicHJvZmlsZSIsInBvc2l0aW9uIjoicGFn

ZUNvbnRlbnQifX0

4. https://dspace.cuni.cz/handle/20.500.11956/64325

5. https://dspace.cuni.cz/handle/20.500.11956/64325

6. http://penelope.uchicago.edu/

7. http://penelope.uchicago.edu/

8. https://www.sefaria.org/texts/Talmud/Yerushalmi%00

About the Author

Elizabeth Legge is a Doctor of Medicine candidate at a European university. She achieved her Master's degree in Classical Archaeology at the University of Pisa, Italy and will be pursuing a PhD in the field. She was awarded her Bachelor of Arts in Classical Studies and Bachelor of Sciences in Integrated Sciences at the University of British Columbia, Canada. She has travelled extensively to all continents since childhood and lived in many countries. She is Australian, Canadian and half English.

Don't miss out!

Visit the website below and you can sign up to receive emails whenever Elizabeth Legge publishes a new book. There's no charge and no obligation.

https://books2read.com/r/B-A-YAIAB-BIYQC

BOOKS2READ

Connecting independent readers to independent writers.

Did you love *The Malhata Fortress on the Roman-Judaean Negev Frontier: Associated with a Roman Road, the Frankincense Trail, and a Princely Fugitive?* Then you should read *Agrippa I: A Comprehensive Archaeological Study of the Last King of Roman Judaea and a True Crime Inquiry*[1] by Elizabeth Legge!

[2]

Agrippa I: A Comprehensive Archaeological Study of the Last King of Roman Judaea and a True Crime Inquiry

Delve into the fascinating world of Agrippa I, the last king of Roman Judaea, through this meticulously researched and riveting exploration. Written by a classical archaeologist and doctor of medicine candidate with prior degrees in classical studies and the biological sciences, this book offers a comprehensive archaeological study of Agrippa I's reign, revealing the historical, political, and cultural intricacies of his time.

---

1. https://books2read.com/u/bo5lG9

2. https://books2read.com/u/bo5lG9

Highlights include:

An in-depth analysis of Agrippa I's rise to power and his complex relationships with key Roman figures, including Claudius and Caligula.A groundbreaking archaeological investigation into the true crime events that shaped Agrippa I's life, with new interpretations of ancient sources including Josephus. uncovering secrets and mysteries long buried in history.Visual insights through architectural remains, coinage, and other artifacts compared against the ancient historical record, with research involving a perusal of over 200 ancient and scholarly sources.

First published as a Classical Archaeology Master's thesis by the University of Pisa, this work achieved full grades and now provides an in-depth understanding of one of history's most intriguing figures. Perfect for scholars, history enthusiasts, and true crime aficionados alike, this book promises to illuminate the past with fresh perspective and scholarly rigour.

Also by Elizabeth Legge

Echoes of Ancient Rome: Politics, Medicine, and War
Woman Physicians in Ancient Rome
The Structure and Phases of the Castra Praetoria in Rome
Roman Military Medicine from an Archaeological and Historical
Perspective
Gaius Caligula's Reign, Personality and Friendship with M. Julius
Agrippa I
The Malhata Fortress on the Roman-Judaean Negev Frontier:
Associated with a Roman Road, the Frankincense Trail, and a Princely
Fugitive
Agrippa I: A Comprehensive Archaeological Study of the Last King of
Roman Judaea and a True Crime Inquiry

Roman Provincial Shadows: Agrippa I, Intrigue, and Power
Herodian Agrippa I Archaeology: Introduction
Historical Background for Herodian Agrippa I
Fugitive Prince: The Negev Hideout of Agrippa I at Malhata
Examples for Comparison from Herod I's Archaeological Record
Agrippa I: An Archaeological Biography of the Last King of Roman
Judaea
Agrippa I's Last Days

Herodian Agrippa I Archaeology: Discussion, Conclusion and Reference List

About the Author

Elizabeth Legge is a Doctor of Medicine candidate at a European university. She achieved her Master's degree in Classical Archaeology at the University of Pisa, Italy and will be pursuing a PhD in the field. She was awarded her Bachelor of Arts in Classical Studies and Bachelor of Sciences in Integrated Sciences at the University of British Columbia, Canada. She has travelled extensively to all continents since childhood and lived in many countries. She is Australian, Canadian and half English.

Read more at https://www.linkedin.com/in/e-l-87b50293/.

www.ingramcontent.com/pod-product-compliance
Lightning Source LLC
Chambersburg PA
CBHW022103150726
47990CB00003B/1227